Wholly Frijoles!

THE WHOLE BEAN COOK BOOK

by

Shayne Fischer

GOLDEN WEST ☼ PUBLISHERS

Cover art by Kris Steele

Other books by Shayne Fischer:

> *Low Fat Mexican Recipes*
>
> *Vegi-Mex Mexican Recipes*

Anasazi Beans® is trademarked to Adobe Milling Co., Inc., Dove Creek, CO

Library of Congress Cataloging-in-Publication Data
Fischer, Shayne
  Wholly Frijoles! / by Shayne Fischer
      p.   cm.
  Includes index.
    1. Cookery (Beans)   2. Cookery, American — Southwestern style I. Title
  ISBN # 1-885590-01-6
  TX803.B4F57 1994   95-49
  641.6'565—dc20   CIP

Printed in the United States of America

ISBN #1-885590-01-6

4th Printing ©1997

Golden West Publishers, Inc.
4113 N. Longview Ave.
Phoenix, AZ 85014, USA
(602) 265-4392

Table of Contents

SOUPS

MAIN DISHES

SIDE DISHES

DESSERTS

Wholly Frijoles!

Introduction

In Spanish the word for bean is frijole (free-ho-lee). This cook book features bean recipes from the southwest and the entire country. The tasty and nutritious recipes throughout **Wholly Frijoles!** show that beans are more than just a side dish or a filler. In fact, beans can be used in appetizers, breads, salads, soups, main dishes, side dishes and even desserts! I haven't come across any bean drinks yet but you can be sure if I do they'll be in the next edition of this book!

Beans are legumes (leg yooms), the seed pods of any of the plants that belong to the pea or Leguminosae family. The pod, such as that of the pea or bean, splits into two valves with the seeds attached to the lower edge of one of the valves.

Legumes grow in most parts of the world and make up the second largest family of flowering plants. Botanists recognize over 13,000 species of legumes which vary widely and may be found in the form of trees, shrubs or herbs. Many are climbing plants. Such legumes as peas, beans and peanuts are very valuable as nutritional foods, providing protein, calcium, phosphorous, vitamins and other nutrients. Alfalfa and clover are important pasture plant legumes. Other types of leguminous plants yield medicines, dyes and oils.

While many types of beans are cultivated throughout the world, varieties of the kidney bean are the most important in the United States and Canada.

Kidney beans were first cultivated by the Indians of South and Central America. Among the many varieties of the kidney bean are the red kidney, the mottled pinto and the white navy. Navy beans became internationally known for their use in Boston baked beans.

Kidney beans have a much greater food value than most of the other legumes. Dry beans are very rich in protein, carbohydrates and fiber and are often eaten as a substitute for meat.

Lima beans are large, flat, white beans that can be eaten dried or green (fresh). Limas are considered to be the most nutritious member of the pea family. The large lima bean often grows to be an inch wide and 1/4 inch thick. High in protein and rich in vitamin B, this bean was first found in the southern areas of the United States. Now it is grown in many warm lands. Limas have become an important crop in California, where they are planted in May and ripen around September.

Pinto beans are beige-colored and speckled. These beans are popular in stews, chilis, refried beans and other Mexican dishes.

Soups made from dried beans are among the world's oldest culinary dishes. The cultivation of leguminous plants goes back 4,000 years.

* * *

Beans are easy to prepare if you know what to do! The following cooking tips are also featured throughout this book. Take a few moments to review them and learn the secrets of creating great bean dishes!

• Tenderness can be tested by the old art of "woofing" the beans. Place a few beans on a saucer and blow across them. If they crack they are tender.

• Add acidic ingredients like tomatoes, tomato sauces, vinegar and lemon juice after the beans have already begun to soften. (Acid slows the cooking process as does the calcium in molasses.)

• Most dried beans take from 2 1/2 - 4 hours to cook. It could take longer if cooking with "hard water" (high in mineral content.) Presoak the beans to reduce this time by an hour.

• Beans can be soaked overnight or several hours prior to cooking. Do not salt soaking water as this will make the skin of the beans tough.

• To de-gas beans, add a 1/2 teaspoon of baking soda to the soaking water. Then use this same water for cooking the beans several hours later or the next day. Another method is to discard the soaking water and add fresh cold water before cooking. Discarding the initial water will help reduce the bean sugar. This sugar seems to be the primary culprit in producing digestive discomfort in some indivduals.

• If you forget to soak your beans, use 6 cups of water per 1 pound of beans. Bring to a boil for 2 minutes, then allow to soak for one hour.

• Adding 2 tablespoons of oil to the cooking water prevents foaming.

• Cooking beans in a crockpot takes from 6 to 8 hours or overnight.

• Always keep beans covered with liquid when cooking to prevent them from drying out and getting tough.

• Store legumes in a cool dry place, like airtight bags or jars.

• Never refrigerate dry beans.

• One cup of cooked or canned beans supplies 12 to 15 grams of vegetable protein, depending on the variety.

• Beans contain no cholesterol unless animal fats are added in cooking to season. They are also naturally low in sodium.

• Beans are an excellent source of dietary fiber, protein, vitamins and minerals. They are also very low in fat.

• Experts note that a cup of cooked dried beans everyday can help control cholesterol, lowering LDL's (low density lipoproteins, the "bad" cholesterol), as well as aid in the control of insulin and blood sugar.

Glossary

ANASAZI BEANS®: Versatile, medium-sized red and white beans that are suitable for any bean recipe.

BLACK BEANS: Small black bean with a smoky taste that lends itself to salsas, salads, casseroles, soups and stews.

BLACK-EYED PEAS: Sometimes called "cowpeas," a deep South favorite. Especially good cooked with ham or chicken.

CANNELLINI BEANS: Large white beans that taste similar to green beans when dry. Great in soups.

FAVA BEANS: These were the only beans known in Europe prior to the discovery of the Americas. They can be eaten green or dried. Try them in a cream or tomato sauce.

GARBANZOS: Sometimes referred to as "chickpeas." The nut-like flavor and texture lend the ability to mix with other vegetables.

GREAT NORTHERN BEANS: A larger white bean with a mild taste. Good for making baked beans, soups and salads.

KIDNEY BEANS: Rich maroon color, firm texture and meaty flavor. Great for salads, casseroles and soups.

LENTILS: Olive green in color, these round, flat seeds from the pods of the lentil plant are a great source of protein and fiber.

LIMA BEANS: Referred to as "butter beans" and "the aristocrat of dry beans" because of its large size and buttery flavor. Excellent in casseroles, soups and with smoked meats and cheese.

LIMAS, BABY: Shaped like large limas, but are actually a dry form of fresh green limas. Cooks quickly, mashes easily.

NAVY BEANS: A small white dried bean related to the common kidney bean. It got its name from its use in the U.S. Navy.

PINK BEANS: Fine for chili con carne, BBQ beans or other Mexican-American favorites. Great in soups and stews.

PINTO BEANS: A spotted southwestern favorite. Cooked, mashed and fried again, they have become a Mexican food staple.

RED BEANS: Cousin of the kidney bean. A natural for chili and soups. A colorful addition to three-bean salad.

SMALL WHITE BEANS: This bean is smaller & firmer than the traditional Navy bean, and so it holds its shape better during long, slow cooking and baking.

SOYBEANS: Native to China and India, the bean is a source of oil, flour and a variety of other products.

Yields for Legumes

TYPE OF BEANS (1 cup)   **YIELD (cups cooked)**

Type	Yield
Black Beans	4
Black-Eyed Peas	3 1/2
Garbanzos/Chickpeas	4
Great Northern Beans	4
Kidney Beans	4
Lentils	4 1/2
Lima Beans	2 1/2
Limas, Baby	3 1/2
Navy Beans	4
Pink Beans	4
Pinto Beans	4
Red Beans	4
Small White Beans	4
Split Peas	4 1/2

Dried beans, with the exception of lentils and split peas, should be soaked in water before cooking. When cooking, make sure the beans are always covered with liquid. Cooking times can range from 1/2 hour to over 3 hours depending on size and density of beans and cooking procedure used.

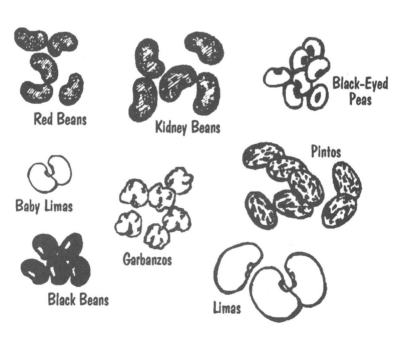

Red Beans

Kidney Beans

Black-Eyed Peas

Baby Limas

Garbanzos

Pintos

Black Beans

Limas

Appetizers

Black Bean Dip

1 (15 oz.) can BLACK BEANS, with juice
2 GARLIC CLOVES
1 Tbsp. VINEGAR
1/2 tsp. SALT
1 Tbsp. SALSA

In a food processor or blender, purée all ingredients together. Serve with your favorite chips, crackers or wedges of pita bread.

Creamy Pinto Bean Dip

I (15 oz.) can REFRIED BEANS
1 (8 oz.) package CREAM CHEESE,
(room temperature)
3 Tbsp. SALSA
1/2 tsp. GARLIC SALT

Blend all of the ingredients thoroughly. Serve with tortilla chips or spread on crisped corn tortillas that have been quartered. These can be heated in a toaster oven or microwave.

Bean & Cheese Dip

2 cups REFRIED BEANS
1 cup shredded LONGHORN CHEESE
2 chopped GREEN ONIONS
3 Tbsp. SALSA

Mix ingredients together and heat thoroughly. This may be done on the stove top, simmering over low heat and stirring often or microwave on medium, stirring occasionally. Serve hot with chips or warmed flour tortillas.

Chunky Bean Dip

1 cup REFRIED BEANS
1/2 cup chopped WALNUTS or PECANS
1 chopped stalk CELERY
2 Tbsp. MAYONNAISE
1/2 tsp. GARLIC SALT

Combine all of the ingredients together and mix well.

Pinto beans are a good source of protein and iron. Adding cheese to your dish provides an even better source of protein.

Spicy Garbanzo Crunchies

These snacks are easy to make and a delicious change from roasted nuts.

1 (15 oz.) can GARBANZO BEANS, drained
1 Tbsp. OIL
1/2 tsp. GARLIC SALT
1/4 tsp. CAYENNE PEPPER
1/4 tsp. CHILI POWDER

Place thoroughly drained garbanzos in a shallow bowl. Coat with oil and seasonings. Mix well making sure that all of the seasonings are well distributed covering the beans. Spread garbanzos in a single layer on a cookie sheet. Bake in a 350 degree oven for 45 minutes or until garbanzos are crunchy.

Acid slows the cooking process, so always wait to add tomatoes or vinegar until beans are almost done. The calcium in molasses has the same effect.

Black Bean Salsa

A Southwestern favorite!

1 (15 oz.) can BLACK BEANS, drained
1 Tbsp. OLIVE OIL
2 peeled and chopped TOMATOES
4 Tbsp. chopped GREEN CHILES
4 diced GREEN ONIONS
1/2 cup chopped fresh CILANTRO
1/8 tsp. GARLIC SALT
1 Tbsp. LEMON JUICE

Combine all of the ingredients together and refrigerate until well chilled.

Bean salsas are especially good served with chicken, pork and beef dishes.

Frijole Dip

2 (15 oz.) cans REFRIED BEANS
1 (8 oz.) container SOUR CREAM
1/2 cup SALSA
1/2 tsp. GARLIC POWDER

Blend all ingredients together until creamy. This dip can be served chilled or can be zapped in the microwave on medium temperature for a couple of minutes. If serving warm, try a little shredded cheese on top. Serve with lots of tortilla chips. This is also great with warmed flour tortillas.

Broiled Falafel Patties

Falafel is a traditional Middle Eastern food.

2 cups cooked GARBANZO BEANS
1/2 cup fresh PARSLEY clusters
1/4 cup BUTTER
2 GARLIC CLOVES
1 EGG, beaten with 1 Tbsp. water
1/2 tsp. DRY MUSTARD
1 tsp. CUMIN
1/2 tsp. CHILI POWDER
1 tsp. WORCESTERSHIRE SAUCE
SALT & PEPPER to taste
OIL as needed

Preheat oven to 350 degrees. Purée the beans and parsley in a blender or food processor, then put mixture in a mixing bowl and add remaining ingredients except for the oil. Mix thoroughly and spoon by tablespoonful onto an oiled baking sheet. Flatten each patty and brush tops with oil. Bake for about 15 minutes or until crispy and golden, or you can broil for a few minutes on each side.

These are great served with a ranch or Thousand Island type of dressing.

Any Bean Salsa

1 (15 oz.) can drained BEANS, (favorite
    bean of choice)
2 lg. diced TOMATOES
1/4 cup diced ONION
1 diced CUCUMBER
4 Tbsp. chopped GREEN CHILES
1/2 cup diced fresh CILANTRO
1/4 tsp. GARLIC SALT
1 Tbsp. LEMON JUICE

Combine all of the ingredients together and chill for one hour.

Lima Snacks

*This is a nutritious and
delicious snack!*

1 (12 oz.) box frozen BABY LIMA BEANS
1 Tbsp. OIL
1/2 tsp. GARLIC SALT

Allow frozen limas to thaw completely on an absorbent towel. In a shallow bowl, toss the lima beans with the oil, coating thoroughly. Spread the coated beans in a single layer on a cookie sheet. Sprinkle with garlic salt and any other seasoning that you favor. Bake in a 350 degree oven for 45 minutes, or until the beans are toasted with a crunchy texture. Serve at room temperature.

Bean Paté

1/2 chopped RED ONION
2 GARLIC CLOVES
1 (16 oz.) can WHITE BEANS (NAVY, GREAT
    NORTHERN, or CANNELINI), drained and
    rinsed
3/4 cup BREAD CRUMBS
1 Tbsp. OLIVE OIL
1 Tbsp. LEMON JUICE
1 tsp. COARSE BROWN MUSTARD
2 Tbsp. PARSLEY
1 Tbsp. chopped fresh BASIL
1/2 tsp. each OREGANO, THYME, DILLWEED
    & TARRAGON
SALT & PEPPER to taste

In a food processor, mince onion and garlic. Add remaining ingredients and process until smooth, stopping once or twice to scrape mixture down the sides of the processor. Taste and adjust seasonings if needed. Cover and refrigerate for at least one hour.

One cup of cooked or canned beans supplies 12 to 15 grams of vegetable protein, depending on the variety.

Bean Balls

3 cups cooked KIDNEY BEANS
1 peeled and cooked POTATO
1 finely chopped ONION
1 stalk finely chopped CELERY
1 tsp. OREGANO
2 minced GARLIC CLOVES
2 Tbsp. chopped fresh PARSLEY
SALT and PEPPER to taste
1/2 cup BREAD CRUMBS

Mash the beans and potato together with a potato masher. Add the onion, celery and herbs and mix well. Form the mixture into 24 small balls. Roll each ball in the bread crumbs and place on a lightly greased baking sheet. Bake at 350 degrees for 30 minutes. Serve with your favorite dressing, dip or salsa.

Breads

Bean-Oat Muffins

1 cup cooked PINTO BEANS
3/4 cup MILK
1 EGG
1/4 cup VEGETABLE OIL
1/2 cup HONEY
1/2 tsp. VANILLA
1 cup FLOUR
3/4 cup QUICK COOKING OATS
1/2 tsp. BAKING SODA
1/2 tsp. CINNAMON
1/2 cup RAISINS

Preheat oven to 400 degrees. Purée beans with milk in a blender until smooth. Pour into a bowl and beat in egg, oil, honey and vanilla. Add in the dry ingredients, mixing until just moistened. Stir in raisins. Spoon into paper-lined muffin cups, about 3/4 full. Bake for 15 to 20 minutes or until golden brown.

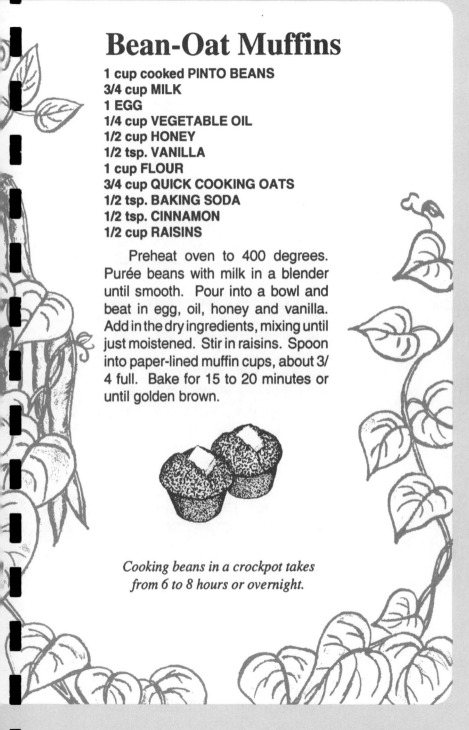

*Cooking beans in a crockpot takes
from 6 to 8 hours or overnight.*

Basic Bean Bread

2 Tbsp. HONEY
1/4 cup HOT WATER
2 Tbsp. plus 3/4 tsp. ACTIVE DRY YEAST
10 to 12 cups WHOLE WHEAT FLOUR
2 cups cooked GREAT NORTHERN BEANS, puréed
1 1/2 cups cooked OATS
1 Tbsp. SALT
1/4 cup OIL

Stir honey into hot water. Let cool to lukewarm (110 degrees). Sprinkle in the yeast and mix to dissolve. Stir in 1 tablespoon of flour, cover and set aside for 10 minutes.

In a large bowl, combine beans, oats, salt and oil. Stir yeast mixture into bean mixture. Stir in enough whole wheat flour to form a stiff dough. If dough is too dry and crumbly, add water a tablespoon at a time until the desired consistency is achieved.

Turn dough out onto a floured surface and knead, working in additional flour as needed, until dough is smooth and elastic, approx. 15 minutes.

Oil your hands, rubbing over the surface of the dough. Cut dough into 4 equal pieces. Cover dough with clean towels, making sure that each piece has room to rise without touching others. Allow bread dough to rise for 45 minutes-1 hour.

(Continued on next page)

Basic Bean Bread *(Continued from page 22)*

Preheat oven to 375 degrees. Lightly oil bread pans. Shape dough into loaves and place in prepared pans. Bake until crust is golden, about 45 minutes. Remove bread from pans and place on wire racks. Let cool for at least 20 minutes before slicing.

This recipe will make four 1 1/2 lb. loaves.

Frijole Loaf

Use the same **Basic Bean Bread** recipe on the previous page. Replace the **GREAT NORTHERN BEANS** with **PINTO BEANS.** Add **1 small can diced GREEN CHILES.**

Banana Nut Loaf

Use the same **Basic Bean Bread** recipe on the previous page. Add to the bean mixture.

2 mashed BANANAS	**2 tsp. VANILLA**
3/4 cup chopped WALNUTS	**1/2 tsp. CINNAMON**

Allow for extra baking time due to moisture content in bananas.

Garbanzo Crackers

1 cup cooked and puréed GARBANZO BEANS
1 tsp. BAKING POWDER
1 EGG
2 Tbsp. VEGETABLE OIL
1 cup FLOUR
3 Tbsp. grated PARMESAN CHEESE
GARLIC SALT

Preheat oven to 425 degrees. Combine all ingredients, but the garlic salt, with a fork or in a food processor until well blended. Roll out to 1/8 inch thick on a floured board. Score into 1 1/2 inch squares. Sprinkle with garlic salt and bake on a cookie sheet for 10 minutes or until golden brown. Cool and break apart at the scored lines.

Legumes provide protein, calcium, phosphorus, vitamins and other nutrients that are vital for good health.

Salads

Beans with Pasta & Veggies

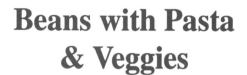

8 oz. uncooked ROTELE PASTA
1 cup cooked NAVY BEANS
1 cup cooked KIDNEY BEANS
1 cup cooked BLACK BEANS
1 sliced RED BELL PEPPER
1 cup sliced CARROTS
1 cup BROCCOLI florets
1/4 cup OLIVE OIL
1/4 cup VINEGAR
1 tsp. SUGAR
1/2 tsp. SALT
1/2 tsp. OREGANO
1/2 tsp. PARSLEY
dash of BLACK PEPPER

Cook pasta according to package directions. Drain and rinse with cold water. Combine all of the ingredients together and chill for at least one hour. Stir gently before serving.

Always keep beans covered with liquid when cooking to prevent them from drying out and getting tough.

Mexican Bean Salad

1 (15 oz.) can KIDNEY BEANS, drained
1 (15 oz.) can PINTO BEANS, drained
1 cup SALSA
1 head shredded LETTUCE
1 cup chopped ONION
1 cup chopped TOMATO
1 cup shredded CHEESE
1 large bag TORTILLA CHIPS

Combine beans and salsa. Place lettuce on plates and top with bean mixture, onion, tomatoes and cheese. Surround with chips and garnish with **SOUR CREAM, GUACAMOLE** and/or **SALSA**.

Black Bean Salad

1 (15 oz.) can BLACK BEANS, drained
3 chopped hard boiled EGGS
1 stalk chopped CELERY
1/3 cup chopped RED ONION
1/2 cup cubed CHEDDAR CHEESE
LETTUCE

Combine all of the ingredients, except for the lettuce. When ready to serve, toss with salad dressing of your choice. Serve on a bed of lettuce.

Calico Beans

1 (15 oz.) can KIDNEY BEANS, drained
1 (15 oz.) can GARBANZO BEANS, drained
1 (15 oz.) can GREAT NORTHERN BEANS, drained
1 chopped RED ONION
1 chopped GREEN BELL PEPPER
1/2 cup SALAD OIL
1/2 cup VINEGAR
1/2 cup SUGAR
1/2 tsp. GARLIC SALT
1/4 tsp. BLACK PEPPER
1/2 tsp. GROUND OREGANO

Combine all of the ingredients together. Refrigerate for a couple of hours. This salad tastes best when marinated overnight. Stir before serving.

Black-Eyed Pea Salad

Try this deliciously different salad!

2 (15 oz.) cans BLACK-EYED PEAS, drained
1 GREEN BELL PEPPER, cut into strips
1 diced TOMATO
1/2 cup chopped RED ONION
1/2 tsp. OREGANO
1/2 cup ITALIAN DRESSING
1 head LETTUCE, torn into pieces

Combine all of the ingredients, except for the lettuce and toss gently. Place lettuce in a large salad bowl and spoon bean mixture over lettuce.

Taco Salad

1 (15 oz.) can PINTO BEANS, drained
1 (15 oz.) can KIDNEY BEANS, drained
1 lb. cooked ground BEEF or TURKEY
1 head LETTUCE, torn into bite-size pieces
1 chopped ONION
2 chopped TOMATOES
1/2 lb. shredded LONGHORN or JACK CHEESE
1 (8 oz.) jar of SALSA
TORTILLA CHIPS

Toss all but the tortilla chips together in a large bowl. Chill. When ready to eat, serve with chips. Some other toppings that go well are **SOUR CREAM, AVOCADO, GREEN CHILES** and **BLACK OLIVES.**

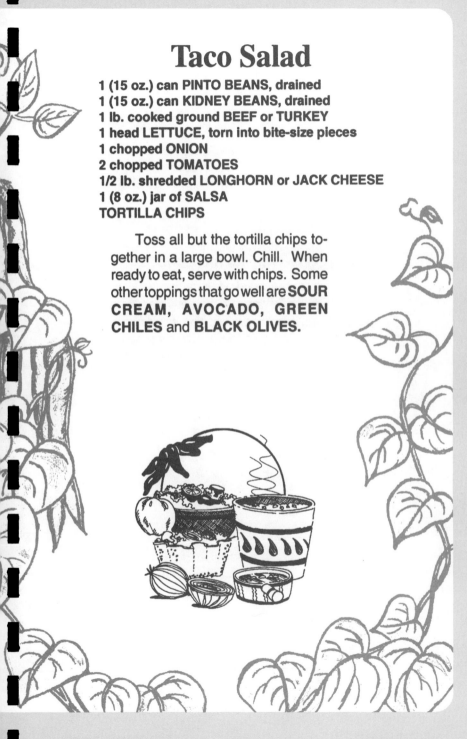

Rotini & Bean Salad

8 oz. uncooked ROTINI PASTA
1 (15 oz.) can KIDNEY BEANS, drained
1 (15 oz.) can GREAT NORTHERN BEANS,
    drained
1 cup BROCCOLI florets
1/2 cup chopped RED BELL PEPPER
1/2 cup sliced BLACK OLIVES
1/2 cup bottled ITALIAN DRESSING

Cook rotini according to package directions. Drain and rinse with cold water. In a large bowl, combine all of the ingredients together. Cover and refrigerate for at least one hour to blend flavors. Toss gently before serving.

To de-gas beans, add a 1/2 teaspoon of baking soda to the soaking water. Then use this same water for cooking the beans.

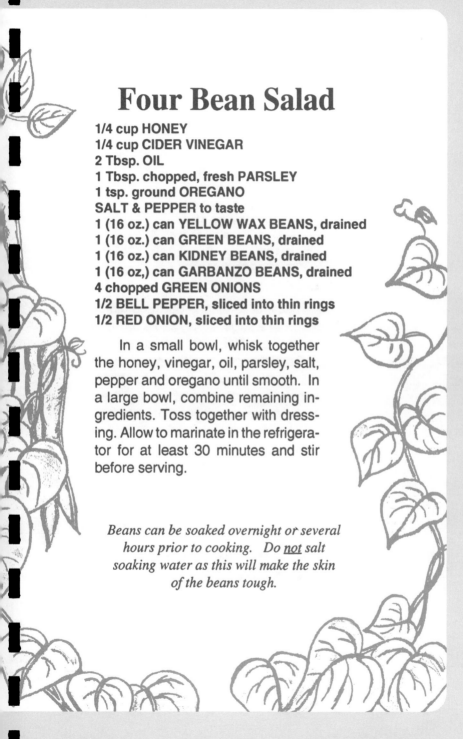

Four Bean Salad

1/4 cup **HONEY**
1/4 cup **CIDER VINEGAR**
2 Tbsp. **OIL**
1 Tbsp. chopped, fresh **PARSLEY**
1 tsp. ground **OREGANO**
SALT & PEPPER to taste
1 (16 oz.) can **YELLOW WAX BEANS**, drained
1 (16 oz.) can **GREEN BEANS**, drained
1 (16 oz.) can **KIDNEY BEANS**, drained
1 (16 oz,) can **GARBANZO BEANS**, drained
4 chopped **GREEN ONIONS**
1/2 **BELL PEPPER**, sliced into thin rings
1/2 **RED ONION**, sliced into thin rings

In a small bowl, whisk together the honey, vinegar, oil, parsley, salt, pepper and oregano until smooth. In a large bowl, combine remaining ingredients. Toss together with dressing. Allow to marinate in the refrigerator for at least 30 minutes and stir before serving.

Beans can be soaked overnight or several hours prior to cooking. Do not salt soaking water as this will make the skin of the beans tough.

Peppy Pasta & Bean Salad

1/2 lb. ROTINI PASTA
1 RED BELL PEPPER, sliced into strips
1/4 cup chopped RED ONION
2 sliced ZUCCHINI
2 minced GARLIC CLOVES
3/4 tsp. ITALIAN SEASONING
1/3 cup and 2 Tbsp. OLIVE OIL
1 (15 oz.) can KIDNEY BEANS
2 Tbsp. minced fresh PARSLEY
juice of 1 LEMON
3/4 tsp. HOT PEPPER SAUCE
SALT & PEPPER to taste

Cook pasta according to package directions, drain. In a large skillet, sauté red bell pepper, onion, zucchini, garlic and Italian seasoning in 2 tablespoons oil until tender but still crisp. Let vegetables cool. In a large bowl, toss pasta, beans and vegetables together. Chill for several hours. Just before serving, whisk together the remaining 1/3 cup of olive oil, parsley, lemon juice, pepper sauce, salt and pepper. Pour over pasta, vegetables and beans; toss to coat thoroughly.

Tuna-Bean Salad

1 (15 oz.) can KIDNEY BEANS, drained
2 (7 oz.) cans TUNA, drained
8 chopped GREEN ONIONS
2 minced GARLIC CLOVES
1 cup OLIVE OIL
1/4 cup VINEGAR
1/4 cup chopped, fresh PARSLEY
SALT & PEPPER to taste
LETTUCE

In a large bowl, combine all ingredients except lettuce. Toss to blend and serve and serve on lettuce leaves. This salad may be served warm or chilled.

Tres Frijoles

(Three Beans)

2 cups cooked KIDNEY BEANS
2 cups cooked BLACK BEANS
2 cups cooked GARBANZO BEANS
1 thinly sliced RED ONION
2 stalks sliced CELERY
1 diced TOMATO
1 cup "mild" THICK & CHUNKY SALSA
shredded LETTUCE

Combine all of the ingredients, except the lettuce, together in a large bowl. Cover and chill for at least one hour. Serve over shredded lettuce.

Zesty Bean Salad

1 (15 oz.) can KIDNEY BEANS, drained
1 (15 oz.) can BLACK BEANS, drained
1 (15 oz.) can PINTO BEANS, drained
1 (4 oz.) can diced GREEN CHILES, drained
4 diced SCALLIONS
1 cup shredded CHEDDAR CHEESE
1 Tbsp. crushed RED PEPPERS
1 pint SOUR CREAM

Combine all ingredients in a large bowl. Refrigerate until well chilled.

Summer Bean Salad

1 (15 oz.) can KIDNEY BEANS, drained
1 (15 oz.) can GREAT NORTHERN BEANS, drained
1/2 cup chopped CELERY
1/2 cup chopped ONION
1 medium-sized, diced CUCUMBER
2 shredded CARROTS
3/4 cup MAYONNAISE
1/4 cup VINEGAR
1/2 cup SUGAR
SALT & PEPPER to taste

Combine all of the ingredients together and mix thoroughly. Allow to chill, preferably overnight. For a heartier salad, add diced, cooked **HAM** and chunks of **CHEESE**.

Garbanzo & Cheese Salad

2 cups cooked **GARBANZO BEANS**
1 cup grated **SWISS CHEESE**
2 cups **RED LEAF LETTUCE**, torn into pieces
1 cup **SPINACH**, torn into pieces
1 cup **ICEBURG LETTUCE**, torn into pieces
3 diced **GREEN ONIONS**
1 sliced **RED BELL PEPPER**
1/2 cup chopped **CUCUMBER**

Toss all of the ingredients together with your favorite salad dressing. Italian works great!

Lentil Salad

1 cup **LENTILS**
1 tsp. **SALT**
1/2 cup **FRENCH DRESSING**
1/4 tsp. **PEPPER**
LETTUCE

Cover lentils in water, add salt and let cook just below boiling point. When tender, drain and add French dressing and pepper. Refrigerate for an hour to absorb dressing. Serve on a bed of lettuce.

Navy Bean Salad

2 1/2 cups dried NAVY BEANS
6 cups WATER
2 stalks diced CELERY
1 chopped ONION
1 chopped GREEN BELL PEPPER
1/2 cup VEGETABLE OIL
1/2 cup VINEGAR
1/2 cup SUGAR
1 tsp. DRY MUSTARD
1 crushed GARLIC CLOVE
1/2 tsp. SALT

Rinse and sort through the beans. Place beans in a saucepan covered with water and let stand overnight. Bring the beans to a boil and cook for approximately 2 hours or until tender. Drain and chill.

Combine the remaining ingredients together and mix well. Toss the salad mixture together with the cooked beans. Chill for at least 4 hours before serving. Garnish with tomato wedges.

Sunshine Salad

2 cups cooked or canned GARBANZO BEANS
1 can whole-kernel CORN, drained
1 cup sliced CELERY
1/2 cup chopped ONION
1/4 cup diced GREEN BELL PEPPER

Combine ingredients and moisten to taste with **Golden Sunshine Dressing.** Chill and serve.

Golden Sunshine Dressing

1/3 cup SUGAR
1/2 tsp. DRY MUSTARD
1 tsp. SALT
2 Tbsp. FLOUR
1 EGG
1/2 cup VINEGAR
1/2 cup WATER
1 Tbsp. BUTTER

Mix dry ingredients. Beat egg with fork in a small bowl. Beat in dry mixture. Heat vinegar, water and butter in a saucepan. Remove from heat and gradually add egg mixture, stirring quickly. Then put back on burner to cook, stirring constantly for 2-3 minutes, until smooth and thick.

Makes 1 1/2 cups of dressing.

Red & Green Salad

This makes a great Christmas salad!

1 can **KIDNEY BEANS**, drained
1 cup frozen **GREEN PEAS**, thawed
1/4 cup chopped **CELERY**
1/4 cup chopped **GREEN BELL PEPPER**
1/4 cup chopped **RED ONION**
1 sm. jar chopped **PIMENTOS**

Mix in a medium sized bowl and set aside.

Dressing:
1/2 cup **VINEGAR**
1/4 cup **VEGETABLE OIL**
1 tsp. **SALT**
1/2 cup **SUGAR**

Mix thoroughly and pour over beans and vegetables. Let sit overnight in the refrigerator. Stir 2 or 3 times. Drain before serving.

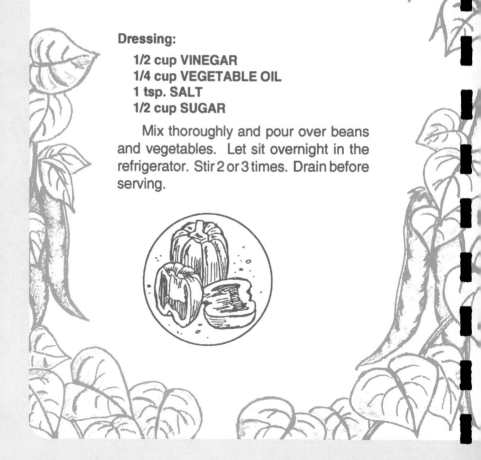

Fiesta Bean Salad

1 (15 oz.) can KIDNEY BEANS, drained
1/2 lb. VELVEETA® CHEESE, cubed
4 chopped HARD-BOILED EGGS
2 stalks chopped CELERY
1 small RED ONION, sliced into rings
1/2 cup THOUSAND ISLAND DRESSING
LETTUCE

Combine all ingredients except for the lettuce. Chill thoroughly. Serve on a bed of lettuce leaves.

Store legumes in a cool dry place,
such as airtight bags or jars.

Zesty Garbanzo Bean Salad

1 (15 oz.) can GARBANZO BEANS, drained
1/4 cup chopped, fresh PARSLEY
2 Tbsp. CHILI SAUCE
1/2 tsp. OREGANO
1/4 cup BOTTLED ITALIAN DRESSING
CRISP SALAD GREENS

Combine all of the ingredients except for the salad greens. Chill thoroughly. Serve on salad greens.

Kidney Beans & Cabbage

This colorful salad is a family favorite!

1/2 lb. BACON
1 chopped ONION
1 cup MAYONNAISE
1/4 cup VINEGAR
2 Tbsp. SUGAR
3 cups shredded CABBAGE
1 cup diced CELERY
2 (16 oz.) cans KIDNEY BEANS, drained
LETTUCE
TOMATO WEDGES

Fry bacon, drain and reserve 1/4 cup of the bacon drippings. Sauté onion in the drippings until limp, remove from the heat. Stir in the mayonnaise, vinegar and sugar. Mix thoroughly. Crumble bacon and add shredded cabbage, celery and beans stirring into the mayonnaise mixture. Serve on crisp lettuce leaves and garnish with tomato wedges.

Garbanzo-Artichoke Salad

1 lb. cooked GARBANZO BEANS (or 2
    cans, well drained)
1 sm. jar marinated ARTICHOKE HEARTS,
    drained and sliced
1 sliced RED BELL PEPPER
1 sliced GREEN BELL PEPPER
1 sliced RED ONION
1 peeled and sliced CUCUMBER
1 shredded CARROT
1/2 cup diced JICAMA
1/2 cup sliced BLACK OLIVES
2 cups shredded LETTUCE
ITALIAN DRESSING

    Combine all of the ingredients together.
Drizzle with your favorite Italian dressing and
toss well.

*1 pound of dry beans = 2 cups dry
beans = 5 to 6 cups cooked beans.*

Soups

Southwestern Navy Bean Soup

1 lb. dried NAVY BEANS, soaked over
    night in 6 cups water
4 cups STOCK or WATER
1 cup chopped ONION
1 cup chopped CELERY
2 Tbsp. OIL or BUTTER
1 can diced GREEN CHILES
dash of CAYENNE PEPPER
SALT & PEPPER to taste
shredded CHEDDAR CHEESE

Drain beans. Put beans and stock in a large soup kettle and bring to a boil. Simmer gently on low heat. Meanwhile, sauté onions and celery in oil until transparent and just beginning to brown. Add to beans. Stir in green chiles. Add enough water to cover the beans by 1 inch. Simmer covered for 1 hour, stirring occasionally and adding more water if necessary. (Beans should always be slightly covered with the simmering broth.) Add cayenne, salt and pepper; cook for another 30 minutes, or until beans are very tender. Garnish with shredded cheese.

Hearty Minestrone

This soup is more like a meal!

2 Tbsp. OLIVE OIL
1 medium ONION, chopped
1 cup chopped CELERY
1 cup chopped CARROTS
1 cup diced POTATOES
1 (16 oz.) can STEWED TOMATOES,
    coarsely chopped
1 (8 oz.) can TOMATO SAUCE
4 cups STOCK or WATER
1 (15 oz.) can KIDNEY BEANS, drained
1 (15 oz.) can GARBANZO BEANS, drained
2 cups shredded CABBAGE
1 cup sliced ZUCCHINI
1/2 tsp. dried OREGANO (or 1 tsp. fresh)
1/2 tsp. dried THYME (or 1 tsp. fresh)
1/2 tsp. dried BASIL (or 1 tsp. fresh)
1/2 cup uncooked ELBOW MACARONI
SALT & PEPPER to taste
grated PARMESAN CHEESE

Put oil in large soup pot and sauté onions, celery, carrots until onions become translucent. Add potatoes, tomatoes, tomato sauce and stock; bring to a boil, then turn down heat and simmer uncovered for 45 minutes. Add beans, cabbage, zucchini, seasonings and macaroni. Cook 15 to 20 minutes or until pasta is done. (Add water if necessary). Top with Parmesan cheese.

Vegetable Bean Soup

2 cups chopped ONION
1 cup chopped CARROTS
1 cup chopped CELERY
3 Tbsp. BUTTER or MARGARINE
5 cups WATER
3 CHICKEN or BEEF BOUILLON CUBES
1 (28 oz.) can TOMATOES, cut up coarsely
1 (15 oz.) can PINTO or BLACK BEANS,
    drained
1 (15 oz.) can GREAT NORTHERN BEANS,
    drained
1 tsp. GARLIC POWDER

In a large saucepan, sauté onion, carrots and celery in butter until onion is translucent. Stir in water, bouillon, tomatoes, beans and garlic powder and bring to a boil. Reduce heat and simmer, covered for 15 minutes or until vegetables are tender.

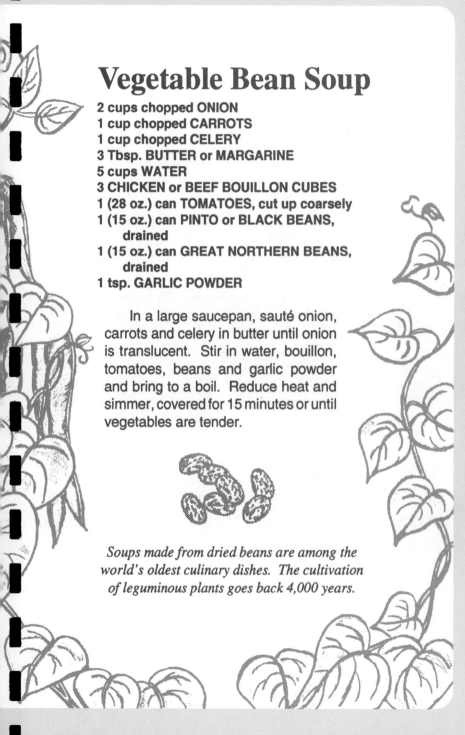

Soups made from dried beans are among the world's oldest culinary dishes. The cultivation of leguminous plants goes back 4,000 years.

Five Bean Soup

1/3 cup GARBANZO BEANS
1/3 cup KIDNEY BEANS
1/3 cup PINTO BEANS
1/3 cup BLACK-EYED PEAS
1/3 cup GREAT NORTHERN BEANS
6 cups WATER
1 chopped ONION
2 diced CARROTS
2 chopped stalks CELERY
2 minced GARLIC CLOVES
1 BAY LEAF
1 cup chopped HAM

Soak beans overnight. Put drained, soaked beans in a large pot with 6 cups of water and remaining ingredients. Bring to a boil. Reduce heat and cover pot, simmer for 3 1/2 hours or until beans are tender.

Tenderness can be tested by the old art of "woofing" the beans. Place a few beans on a saucer and blow across them. If they crack they are tender.

Lentil Soup

*This quick & easy soup tastes great
served with hot buttered corn bread!*

2 cups LENTILS
2 quarts COLD WATER
1 HAM BONE
1 small chopped ONION
2 ribs diced CELERY
1 diced CARROT
SALT & PEPPER to taste

Cook lentils in two quarts cold water
and the rest of the ingredients for about
two hours or until soft. This soup can be
put through a sieve; it is also great with
the lentils left whole.

Lima Bean Soup

1 cup dried LIMA BEANS
1 quart STOCK or WATER
2 ribs chopped CELERY
2 diced CARROTS
1 chopped ONION
2 Tbsp. BUTTER
1 Tsp. SALT

Soak lima beans in 1 quart stock or
water overnight. In the morning, add remaining ingredients. Cover and simmer for
two to three hours or until tender.

Lentil & Rice Soup

This soup can be frozen and reheated with excellent results!

1 chopped ONION
2 stalks chopped CELERY
2 chopped CARROTS
2 minced GARLIC CLOVES
2 Tbsp. BUTTER
8 cups WATER
1 lb. LENTILS
2-3 tsp. SALT
1/4 tsp. PEPPER
1/2 tsp. BASIL
1/2 tsp. OREGANO
1/2 tsp. THYME
1 1/2 cup WATER
1/2 cup RICE

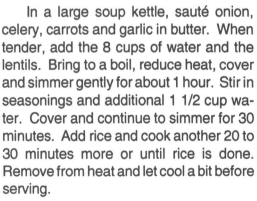

In a large soup kettle, sauté onion, celery, carrots and garlic in butter. When tender, add the 8 cups of water and the lentils. Bring to a boil, reduce heat, cover and simmer gently for about 1 hour. Stir in seasonings and additional 1 1/2 cup water. Cover and continue to simmer for 30 minutes. Add rice and cook another 20 to 30 minutes more or until rice is done. Remove from heat and let cool a bit before serving.

Dried Legume Soup

2 cups of whichever legume you like: Soybeans,
    Pintos, Navy Beans, Limas, Kidneys, Black-eyed
    Peas, Garbanzos, Lentils or a combination
    of any or all of these.
8 cups WATER or STOCK
1 chopped ONION
2 ribs chopped CELERY
2 sliced CARROTS
1 chopped GARLIC CLOVE
1 BAY LEAF

    In a large kettle, soak legumes in water or stock overnight. In the morning add remaining ingredients. Bring to a boil, turn down the heat to a slow simmer. Cover and continue to simmer for 2 or 3 hours or until legumes are tender. Half of the soup can be run through a blender and poured back into the pot to make a creamier soup. If you would like a heartier soup, put a **HAM BONE** or chunked **HAM** in the kettle before cooking but after soaking.

Kidney Bean Soup

This hearty soup will warm any appetite!

2 Tbsp. BUTTER
1 large chopped ONION
2 stalks sliced CELERY
2 sliced CARROTS
2 minced cloves GARLIC
2 (15 oz.) cans KIDNEY BEANS, with liquid
4-6 oz. cubed HAM
4 cups WATER
1 Tbsp. WORCESTERSHIRE SAUCE
2 Tbsp. finely chopped, fresh PARSLEY
1/2 tsp. ground OREGANO
2 BAY LEAVES
1 Tbsp. LEMON JUICE
SALT & PEPPER to taste

In a large saucepan, melt butter. Add onion and sauté until limp. Add celery, carrot and garlic and continue to sauté for a few minutes until soft. Add kidney beans with liquid, ham and water. Bring to a boil. Cook soup for a couple of minutes then add the Worcestershire sauce, parsley, oregano, bay leaves and lemon juice. Bring to a boil again and cook for about 15 minutes. Season with salt and pepper to taste. Remove bay leaves. Serve piping hot.

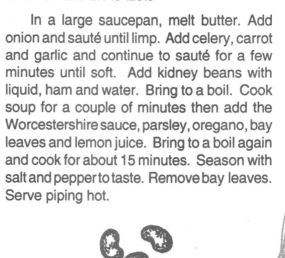

Winter Day Soup

*This thick and chunky soup is well
worth the wait!*

**2 cups mixed dried beans: Great Northern,
Navy, Pinto, Lima, Black, Garbanzo,
Lentils, Split Peas, Black-eyed Peas etc.
2 Tbsp. SALT
2 quarts WATER
2 cups diced HAM or sliced cooked SAUSAGES
1 chopped ONION
1 minced GARLIC CLOVE
1 tsp. CHILI POWDER
1 (28 oz.) can TOMATOES
SALT & PEPPER to taste**

Rinse beans and place in a large
kettle. Cover with water, add salt and
soak overnight. Drain. Add two quarts
of water and meat. Simmer for three
hours. Add onion, garlic, chili powder,
tomatoes and salt & pepper to taste.
Continue simmering for 45 minutes
longer. This soup is great served with
a crusty bread and a green salad.

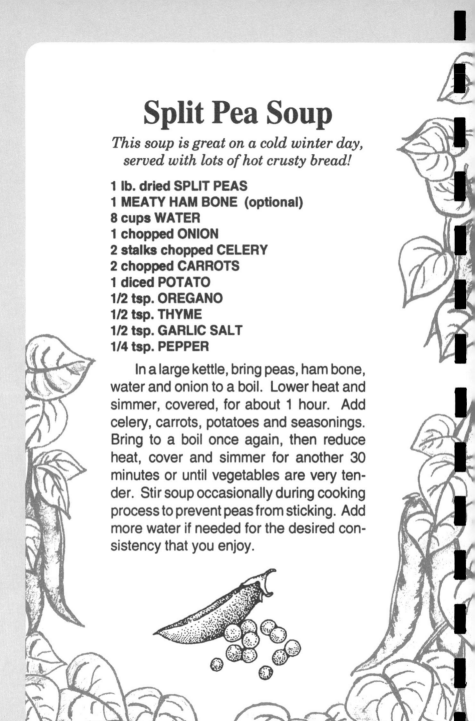

Split Pea Soup

*This soup is great on a cold winter day,
served with lots of hot crusty bread!*

1 lb. dried SPLIT PEAS
1 MEATY HAM BONE (optional)
8 cups WATER
1 chopped ONION
2 stalks chopped CELERY
2 chopped CARROTS
1 diced POTATO
1/2 tsp. OREGANO
1/2 tsp. THYME
1/2 tsp. GARLIC SALT
1/4 tsp. PEPPER

In a large kettle, bring peas, ham bone, water and onion to a boil. Lower heat and simmer, covered, for about 1 hour. Add celery, carrots, potatoes and seasonings. Bring to a boil once again, then reduce heat, cover and simmer for another 30 minutes or until vegetables are very tender. Stir soup occasionally during cooking process to prevent peas from sticking. Add more water if needed for the desired consistency that you enjoy.

Black Bean Soup

This soup is delicious served hot or chilled!

2 (15 oz.) cans BLACK BEANS, drained
2 (15 oz.) cans CHICKEN STOCK
1/2 cup chopped ONION
SALT & PEPPER, to taste
1/2 cup DRY SHERRY
thin slices of LEMON

Combine black beans, chicken stock and onion in a saucepan. Bring to a boil. Cover and simmer on low heat until onion is tender. Add salt and pepper, stir in the sherry. Ladle into bowls and garnish with lemon slices.

To de-gas beans, discard the soaking water and add fresh cold water before cooking. Discarding the initial water will help reduce the bean sugar. This sugar seems to be the primary culprit in producing digestive discomfort in some individuals.

Bean & Split Pea Soup

1/2 cup each: dried **Kidney Beans, Navy Beans, Pinto Beans** and **Black-Eyed Peas**
1/2 cup each: **YELLOW SPLIT PEAS** and **GREEN SPLIT PEAS**
9 cups cold **WATER** or **STOCK**
3 Tbsp. **BUTTER**
2 thinly sliced **ONIONS**
2 thinly sliced **CARROTS**
4 thinly sliced stalks **CELERY**
1 crushed clove **GARLIC**
1 lb. **POLISH SAUSAGE (Kielbasa)**
1 (28 oz.) can **WHOLE TOMATOES**
BLACK PEPPER, to taste

Wash beans and peas. Soak overnight covered in water. Replace soaking water with fresh water or stock. Bring to a boil, then turn down heat to simmer for an hour or until beans are tender.

While pot is simmering, melt the butter in a large skillet and add onions, carrots, celery and garlic. Cover and cook gently until onions are translucent. Add vegetables to bean and pea mixture. Thinly slice the sausage and brown in the skillet. Remove with a slotted spoon and add to soup pot. Add tomatoes (with liquid) and pepper to taste. Let simmer until ready to serve. Ladle into heated bowls and serve with bread and a green salad.

Main Dishes

Chalupa

*This chunky combination makes great
tostadas and burros!*

3 lbs. PORK ROAST, trimmed of all fat
1 lb. PINTO BEANS, washed
2 GARLIC CLOVES, chopped
2 Tbsp. CHILI POWDER
1 Tbsp. ground CUMIN
1 Tbsp. OREGANO
1 (4 oz.) can chopped GREEN CHILES
1 Tbsp. SALT

Place all ingredients in a large pot, kettle, or crock pot and cover with water. Simmer over low heat, adding water if needed. After 6 hours, remove bones and break up roast. Continue cooking with lid off until thick. Serve on tostada shells with chopped lettuce, onion, tomatoes, avocado and cheese. Or, roll up a generous amount in a large warm flour tortilla, like a burro. Chalupa freezes perfectly!

Experts note that a cup of cooked dried beans everyday can help control cholesterol, lowering LDL's (low density lipoproteins, the "bad" cholesterol), as well as aid in the control of insulin and blood sugar.

Refried Anasazi Beans®

1 lb. dried ANASAZI BEANS®
6 cups WATER
1/4 cup finely chopped ONION
1 clove GARLIC, crushed
6 slices chopped BACON
1/4 cup finely chopped GREEN PEPPER
1 tsp. CHILI POWDER

In a saucepan, combine beans and water and cook at a gentle boil for 1 1/2 hours or until tender. Drain beans, reserving liquid. In a skillet, sauté onion, pepper, garlic and bacon. Add sautéed ingredients to beans and mash all together, adding liquid a little at a time, until mixture is smooth in consistancy. Serve with tortillas or cornbread.

Note: These refried beans may be frozen for later use.

Anasazi Beans® do not need pre-soaking, cook faster, and are much sweeter than any other bean.

Beans & Bow Ties

8 oz. BOW TIE PASTA
2 Tbsp. BUTTER
1 chopped ONION
1 chopped GREEN BELL PEPPER
1 (15 oz.) can KIDNEY BEANS, drained
**1 (15 oz.) can GREAT NORTHERN
     BEANS, drained**
1/2 tsp. OREGANO
1/2 tsp. GARLIC SALT
1/4 tsp. PEPPER

Cook pasta according to package directions. Drain and rinse with cool water. In a skillet, melt butter and sauté onion until it becomes translucent. Add green pepper and sauté 2 minutes. Add beans, pasta and seasonings. Simmer on low, heat thoroughly and serve warm.

• For a heartier meal, add **GROUND BEEF, TURKEY** or any leftover meats.

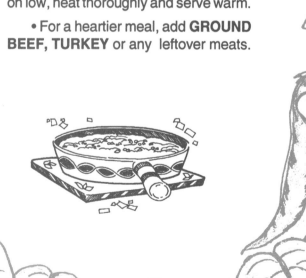

Frijole Stuffed Peppers

This is a unique Mexican version of stuffed peppers.

2 cups cooked PINTO BEANS or REFRIED BEANS
2 Tbsp. OIL
1 chopped ONION
1 cup chopped CELERY
1 cup "mild" THICK & CHUNKY SALSA
1 (12 oz.) can CORN, drained
6 GREEN BELL PEPPERS, seeded and membranes removed
1 cup shredded JACK or CHEDDAR CHEESE

Preheat oven to 400 degrees. Mash beans. Heat oil in a skillet and sauté onion and celery. Stir in salsa, corn and mashed beans. Fill peppers with stuffing and top with cheese. Place stuffed peppers in a pan, adding an inch of water to keep peppers from burning or drying out. Bake for 1/2 hour, replenishing water in pan if necessary.

If you forget to soak your beans, use 6 cups of water per 1 pound of beans. Bring to a boil for 2 minutes, then allow to soak for one hour. Adding 2 tablespoons of oil to the cooking water prevents foaming.

Tostadas

OIL for frying
5 cups cooked or canned PINTO BEANS
SALT to taste
1 dozen CORN TORTILLAS

Garnishes:
   shredded JACK or CHEDDAR CHEESE
   shredded LETTUCE
   chopped TOMATOES
   chopped ONION
   SALSA
   SOUR CREAM

In a deep, heavy skillet, heat enough oil to cover bottom of pan. Oil should be very hot but not smoking. Add the beans and, using a wooden spoon, mash the beans against the skillet. The oil should be hot enough to fry the beans. Salt to taste.

Next, fry the tortillas briefly in a little bit of oil, or crisp in a hot oven. To assemble, spread a generous amount of refried beans on each tortilla. Add garnishes, putting the cheese on top of the hot beans to melt, then lettuce, tomato and whatever other toppings you like. **BLACK OLIVES** and **AVOCADO SLICES** add good flavor and color.

One tostada includes each of the basic four food groups: Beans and cheese for protein and calcium. The tortilla shell supplies B vitamins, and the lettuce, tomatoes and chile provide vitamins A and C.

South of the Border Bean Bake

OIL for sautéing
1 chopped ONION
2 EGGS
2 cups MILK
1 cup shredded CHEDDAR CHEESE
1 cup PINTO BEANS, canned or cooked
1 cup KIDNEY BEANS, canned or cooked
1 (4 oz.) can diced GREEN CHILES
6 CORN TORTILLAS, cut into strips
1/2 cup grated JACK or CHEDDAR CHEESE
1 cup chopped TOMATOES

Preheat oven to 350 degrees. Heat oil and sauté onions until they are translucent. Beat eggs in a bowl and add milk, shredded cheddar cheese, beans, green chiles and sautéed onion. Line the bottom and sides of a glass casserole dish with tortilla strips and fill with bean mixture from the bowl. Sprinkle the top with the grated cheese and tomatoes. Bake for about 45 minutes or until it is firm in the middle and brown on top.

The word "protein" comes from a Greek word meaning "to take first place".

Frijole Steaks

4 MINUTE STEAKS
1 (15 oz.) can REFRIED BEANS
1/4 cup chopped ONIONS
1/4 cup SALSA
1/4 cup BARBECUE SAUCE

Combine beans, onions, salsa and barbecue sauce in a bowl. Place equal amounts of bean mixture on steaks, roll up and secure with wooden toothpicks or skewers. Brush with more barbecue sauce. Broil for a few minutes, turn and continue cooking until steaks are done.

Easy Chili

1 lb. lean GROUND BEEF
1 (15 oz.) can PINTO BEANS, drained
1 chopped ONION
1 (15 oz.) can chopped STEWED
TOMATOES
1 minced GARLIC CLOVE
2 Tbsp. CHILI POWDER
1 tsp. ground CUMIN
1/4 tsp. ground ALLSPICE

Brown ground beef, drain any excess fat. Add remaining ingredients and simmer together for 20-30 minutes.

Pollo con Frijoles Negro
(Chicken with Black Beans)

4 half cooked CHICKEN BREASTS
2 cups cooked BLACK BEANS
1/2 cup SALSA
1/2 cup WHITE WINE
1/4 tsp. GARLIC POWDER
SALT & PEPPER to taste

Place chicken breasts on dinner plates. In a bowl, combine beans, salsa, wine and garlic powder. Top each chicken serving with the bean mixture. Season to taste. Heat in microwave on medium-high setting until thoroughly cooked. Serve hot.

Hearty Bean Pie

1 lb. GROUND BEEF or TURKEY
1 Tbsp. WORCESTERSHIRE SAUCE
1/2 tsp. SEASONING SALT
1 (16 oz.) can PORK & BEANS
1 (16 oz.) can TOMATOES
1/4 lb. BACON
1/2 cup BROWN SUGAR

Brown meat and drain off the fat. Add Worcestershire sauce and seasoning salt. Spoon mixture into bottom of a 9 inch pie pan. Mix beans and tomatoes and spoon over meat. Lay bacon strips on top of bean mixture and sprinkle on brown sugar. Bake at 350 degrees for 45 minutes.

Bean & Lentil Stew

1 cup dried LENTILS, rinsed and drained
1 (15 oz.) can GARBANZO BEANS, undrained
2 cups cubed POTATOES
1 cup sliced CARROTS
2 stalks sliced CELERY
1 chopped ONION
1 chopped GREEN BELL PEPPER
1 (28 oz.) can STEWED TOMATOES, cut up
1 tsp. GARLIC SALT
1/4 tsp. PEPPER
1 1/2 Tbsp. CHILI POWDER

In a large saucepan or Dutch oven, combine all of the ingredients and mix well. Bring to a boil. Reduce heat, cover and simmer for 45 minutes to an hour or until vegetables and lentils are tender.

Add acidic ingredients like tomatoes, tomato sauces, vinegar and lemon juice after the legumes have already begun to soften. Even though lentils and split peas do not require soaking, natural acid will keep all legumes from softening properly.

Southwestern Bean & Burger

1 lb. lean GROUND BEEF
1 chopped ONION
2 cups cooked KIDNEY BEANS
2 cups cooked PINTO BEANS
2 cups cooked NAVY BEANS
2 tsp. WORCESTERSHIRE SAUCE
4 Tbsp. KETCHUP
2 tsp. PREPARED MUSTARD
2 Tbsp. BROWN SUGAR
1 tsp. CHILI POWDER
1 tsp. GARLIC SALT
1/4 tsp. PEPPER
1/4 tsp. ground OREGANO

In a large skillet or Dutch oven, cook ground beef and onions over medium heat until the meat is browned and the onions are translucent. Drain and add all of the remaining ingredients. Mix thoroughly, cover and simmer on low heat, stirring occasionally for approximately 20 minutes or until heated completely.

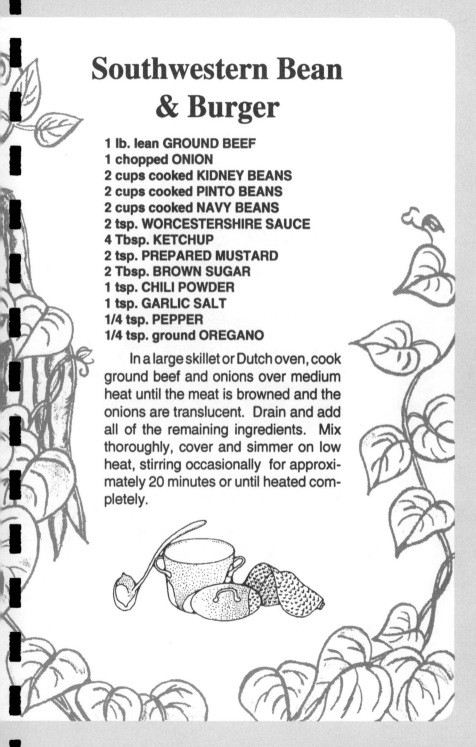

Bean & Beef Casserole

1/2 lb. sliced BACON, diced
1 lb. lean GROUND BEEF
1 chopped ONION
1 (15 oz.) can KIDNEY BEANS, rinsed
    and drained
1 (15 oz.) can LIMA BEANS, rinsed
    and drained
1 (15 oz.) can PORK AND BEANS
1/2 cup BARBECUE SAUCE
1/2 cup KETCHUP
2 Tbsp. MUSTARD
2 Tbsp. WORCESTERSHIRE SAUCE
3/4 cup packed BROWN SUGAR
3 Tbsp. MOLASSES
1/2 tsp. GARLIC SALT
1/2 tsp. CHILI POWDER

Fry bacon, beef and onion until meat is browned and onion is translucent. Drain. In a greased casserole dish combine meat and onion mixture with all of the beans. In a separate bowl, blend the remaining ingredients together. Stir this sauce into the bean and beef mixture. Cover and bake for 45 minutes in a 350 degree oven. Remove cover and bake an additional 15 minutes.

Note: Any variety of beans may be used, try **BLACK BEANS** or **GARBANZO BEANS** for a distinctively different taste.

Black-Eyed Pea Casserole

1 1/2 lbs. GROUND ROUND
1 large chopped ONION
2 minced GARLIC CLOVES
1 (15 oz.) can BLACK-EYED PEAS WITH
    JALAPEÑOS, drained
1 (14 oz.) can ENCHILADA SAUCE
1 (15 oz.) can STEWED TOMATOES
1 can CREAM OF MUSHROOM SOUP
1 can CREAM OF CHICKEN SOUP
1 dozen CORN TORTILLAS, cut into wedges
2 cups shredded CHEDDAR CHEESE

In a skillet, fry ground round, onion and garlic until browned. Drain. Add black-eyed peas, enchilada sauce, tomatoes and both soups. Layer meat mixture, cheese and tortillas in a greased casserole dish. Topping off with the shredded cheese. Bake in a preheated 350 degree oven for 30 minutes or until bubbly.

Note: This casserole can be made with **GROUND TURKEY** and substitute any of your favorite legumes in place of the black-eyed peas.

Beans contain no cholesterol unless animal fats are added in cooking to season. They are also naturally low in sodium.

Spicy Turkey with Beans

1 lb. GROUND TURKEY
1 large chopped ONION
2 minced GARLIC CLOVES
1 Tbsp. VEGETABLE OIL
1 tsp. GROUND CUMIN
1/2 tsp. each SALT and PEPPER
1 (28 oz.) can cut up WHOLE TOMATOES
1 (15 oz.) can TOMATO SAUCE
1 (4 oz.) can diced GREEN CHILES
1 (15 oz.) can KIDNEY BEANS, drained
1 (15 oz.) can GREAT NORTHERN BEANS,
    drained

In a large saucepan cook turkey, onion and garlic in hot oil over medium heat until turkey is no longer pink and onion is translucent. Drain off any excess fat. Add cumin, salt and pepper. Stir and cook for a minute more. Stir in undrained tomatoes, tomato sauce and green chiles. Bring to a boil. Reduce heat, cover and simmer for 20 minutes, stirring occasionally. Add beans and heat through. Ladle into serving bowls and garnish with **SOUR CREAM, SHREDDED CHEESE** and chopped **GREEN ONION.**

Beans are an excellent source of dietary fiber, protein, vitamins and minerals. They are also very low in fat.

Spicy Microwave Chili

2 lbs. crumbled GROUND BEEF
1 chopped ONION
1 chopped BELL PEPPER
1 (15 oz.) can KIDNEY BEANS, drained
1 (6 oz.) can TOMATO SAUCE
1 (29 oz.) can chopped TOMATOES
1 tsp. GARLIC SALT
2-3 Tbsp. CHILI POWDER
1/8 tsp. CAYENNE PEPPER

Brown ground beef in a glass baking dish in microwave for 6-7 minutes on HIGH, stirring twice. Drain off any excess fat. Cook onion and bell pepper in 2 tablespoons of water in a microproof bowl for 2 minutes on HIGH. Combine with meat and remaining ingredients, mixing thoroughly. Microwave on HIGH for 12 minutes, stirring once. Let stand covered for 5 minutes before serving. Garnish with a dollop of **SOUR CREAM** and shredded **CHEDDAR CHEESE.**

Black Bean & Brown Rice Burritos

1 (15 oz.) can BLACK BEANS, drained
1 finely grated, large ONION
1 (4 oz.) can diced GREEN CHILES
2 Tbsp. chopped fresh CILANTRO
1 tsp. RED CHILI POWDER
8 WHOLE WHEAT FLOUR TORTILLAS
2 cups cooked BROWN RICE
SALT & PEPPER to taste
1 cup SALSA

Preheat oven to 350 degrees. In a large mixing bowl, mash beans with grated onion. Stir in the chiles, cilantro and chili powder. Spread tortillas out on a counter and place equal amounts of the bean mixture on each. Top each with 1/4 cup of cooked brown rice. Fold in sides and roll tortilla to completely enclose contents. Place all eight burritos, seam side down, in a non-stick baking pan. Pour salsa evenly over the burritos and bake at 350 degrees for 20 minutes.

Garnish with **SHREDDED CHEESE, SOUR CREAM** and/or **GUACAMOLE.**

Beans & Kielbasa

1 lb. SMOKED KIELBASA SAUSAGE
1 chopped ONION
2 minced GARLIC CLOVES
3 ribs sliced CELERY
2 (15 oz.) cans GREAT NORTHERN
    BEANS, drained
1 (15 oz.) can KIDNEY BEANS, drained
1 (15 oz.) can STEWED TOMATOES
1/2 tsp. OREGANO
1/2 tsp. THYME
1/2 tsp. ROSEMARY
1 Tbsp. BROWN SUGAR

Brown sausage in a large saucepan or Dutch oven. Remove sausage and set aside, reserving 1 teaspoon of the drippings. Add onion, garlic and celery to the drippings and cook until tender-crisp. Add sausage and the rest of the ingredients. Bring to a boil. Lower heat, cover and simmer for 15 minutes. This dish is great served with a green salad and slices of crusty bread.

Dry beans offer the body fuel in the form of carbohydrates to stoke the human engine. Since they digest slowly, they help to satisfy hunger over a long period of time. In addition they help the body use fat efficiently, thus making the most of the protein that they offer.

Bean Enchiladas

These flat enchiladas are similar to a tostada.

2 cups MASA HARINA (corn flour)
1 EGG
1 tsp. BAKING POWDER
1/2 cup VEGETABLE OIL
2 cups shredded LONGHORN CHEESE
WATER

Combine all ingredients, except for water, in a large bowl. Add enough water to make a stiff dough. Let the dough rest for 15 minutes. Form into 1/2 inch thick, round cakes about the size of a hamburger patty. Fry in a small amount of oil in a skillet until browned. Drain on paper towels. Top with a healthy spread of **REFRIED BEANS**. Follow with toppings of your choice:

- **ENCHILADA SAUCE**
- **SHREDDED CHEESE**
- **SHREDDED LETTUCE**
- **CHOPPED ONION**
- **DICED GREEN CHILES**
- **SALSA**
- **SOUR CREAM**
- **GUACAMOLE**
- **BLACK OLIVES**

Black Bean Chili

1 lb. GROUND BEEF
2 Tbsp. OIL
1 chopped ONION
1 chopped BELL PEPPER
2 crushed GARLIC CLOVES
1 lb. BLACK BEANS, soaked, cooked
    and drained
2 Tbsp. hot CHILI POWDER
1 tsp. CUMIN
1 Tbsp. WORCESTERSHIRE SAUCE
1 (28 oz.) can TOMATOES, cut up
SALT & PEPPER to taste

Brown ground beef in oil along with onion, bell pepper and garlic. Drain excess fat and add all of the remaining ingredients. Simmer for at least 1 1/2 hours or until beans are tender.

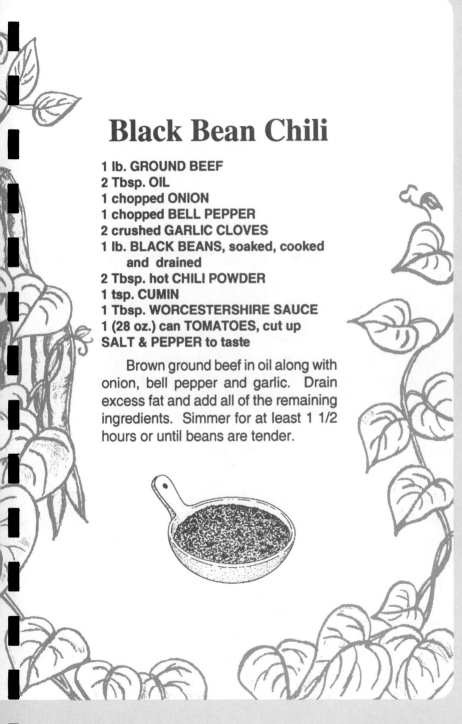

Spicy Vegetable Chili

1 1/2 cup sliced ONIONS
1 1/2 cup sliced CELERY
1 1/2 cup sliced GREEN BELL PEPPER
4 cloves minced GARLIC
2 Tbsp. BUTTER
2 (28 oz.) cans chopped WHOLE
    TOMATOES (reserve juice)
3 (15 1/2 oz.) cans KIDNEY BEANS
1 (15 oz.) can GREAT NORTHERN BEANS
1 Tbsp. CHILI POWDER
1 Tbsp. chopped PARSLEY
2 tsp. SALT
1 tsp. BASIL
1 tsp. OREGANO
1/2 tsp. PEPPER
1/4 tsp. TABASCO® SAUCE
1/4 cup VINEGAR
2 cups shredded CHEDDAR CHEESE

Sauté onion, celery, green pepper and garlic in butter until tender. Stir in tomatoes, tomato juice, and the undrained kidney and great northern beans. Add remaining ingredients, except cheese. Bring to a boil, reduce heat and cover. Simmer for 1 hour. Remove cover and simmer 1 hour longer. Ladle into serving dishes and top with 1/4 cup shredded cheese.

Bean Burgers

*This makes a great vegetarian
alternative to hamburgers!*

**3 cups cooked KIDNEY or PINTO
    BEANS
1 finely chopped ONION
1 cooked POTATO
2 chopped TOMATOES
1 minced clove GARLIC
1 tsp. OREGANO
1 tsp. THYME
3/4 cup BREADCRUMBS
SALT and PEPPER to taste**

    Mix all ingredients thoroughly, either in a food processor or with potato masher. If mixture is too wet, add more breadcrumbs. Form into eight burgers and place them on a lightly greased baking tray. Bake at 350 degrees for 30 minutes, turn and cook an additional 15 minutes. Serve on hamburger buns with onions, lettuce, tomatoes, pickles and your favorite condiments.

Side Dishes

Hoppin' John Peas

This dish is normally made with red beans. The black-eyed peas add a distinctively different flavor.

2 cups dried BLACK-EYED PEAS
1 meaty HAM BONE
1 chopped ONION
1 minced GARLIC CLOVE
1 tsp. SALT
1/4 tsp. PEPPER
1 cup INSTANT RICE
1 (16 oz.) can STEWED TOMATOES

Cover black-eyed peas with water and bring to a boil. Add ham bone, onion, garlic, salt and pepper. Cover and simmer for 1 hour and 30 minutes. Remove ham bone. Pour rice on top of the black-eyed peas and add enough water just to cover the rice. Bring to a boil, cover and remove from heat. Let stand covered for 15 minutes to allow the rice to cook. Stir in the tomatoes, warm, and serve.

"Beans are worth their weight in protein", says a recent release from the USDA. A cup of cooked or canned beans supplies about 12 to 15 grams of vegetable protein, depending on variety.

Black-Eyed Peas & Ham Hocks

*A traditional "Good Luck" dish
for the New Year!*

2 cups dried BLACK-EYED PEAS
4 SMOKED HAM HOCKS
1 chopped ONION
2 stalks chopped CELERY
1 Tbsp. CRUSHED RED PEPPER
2 BAY LEAVES
1 tsp. GARLIC SALT
1/2 tsp. SUGAR
1 tsp. DRY MUSTARD
SALT & PEPPER to taste

Soak peas overnight. Place ham hocks in a large pot and add enough water to cover. Bring to a boil, reduce heat and simmer for 30 minutes. Add black-eyed peas and all of the other ingredients. Simmer until peas are tender and the liquid is almost absorbed. Serve with hot corn bread.

Tangy Black-Eyed Peas

2 cups BLACK-EYED PEAS
1 chopped RED ONION
1 minced GARLIC CLOVE
1 tsp. WORCESTERSHIRE SAUCE
2 Tbsp. BUTTER
SALT & PEPPER to taste

Cover the black-eyed peas with water and add onion and garlic. Bring to a boil, reduce heat to a simmer. Cover and cook for 1 hour or until peas are tender. Add remaining ingredients and cook uncovered on low heat for another 15 minutes.

Cowboy Beans

2 (18 oz.) cans PORK & BEANS
1/2 cup chopped ONION
1 tsp. finely chopped JALAPEÑO PEPPER
1 cup KETCHUP
1/2 cup BROWN SUGAR
2 Tbsp. WORCESTERSHIRE SAUCE
1 Tbsp. MUSTARD
2 strips BACON

Mix all ingredients together except for bacon. Pour into a 2 quart casserole dish. Top with bacon. Bake at 350 degrees for 1 hour. Remove bacon and crumble on top. Stir before serving.

Black-Eyed Peas & Brown Rice

3 cups cooked BLACK-EYED PEAS
1 cup cooked BROWN RICE
1 cup cooked diced MEAT
2 cups CHICKEN STOCK
2 Tbsp. chopped PARSLEY
SALT and PEPPER to taste

Combine cooked peas and rice with other ingredients, heat thoroughly and serve.

Black-eyed peas are also known as "cowpeas".

Chile-Peas

Try this zesty Southwestern dish!

4 cups cooked BLACK-EYED PEAS
1 (4 oz.) can diced GREEN CHILES
4 sliced GREEN ONIONS
1 (15 oz.) can STEWED TOMATOES
1 minced GARLIC CLOVE
1/4 tsp. ground OREGANO
1/4 tsp. each SALT & PEPPER

Drain and chop the tomatoes. Combine all ingredients in a bowl. This dish can be served hot or chilled. If serving cold, add 2 tsp. each of **OIL & VINEGAR**, and refrigerate for 2-3 hours. If serving as a hot dish, simmer on low heat until thoroughly warmed or microwave covered on medium for 5 minutes.

Mexicali Chickpeas

1 lb. cooked CHICKPEAS (Garbanzo Beans)
    or 2 (16 oz.) cans, well drained
1 thinly sliced RED ONION
1 coarsely chopped GREEN BELL PEPPER
1 coarsely chopped RED BELL PEPPER
1/4 cup sliced BLACK OLIVES
1 (4 oz.) can diced GREEN CHILES

Dressing:
    1 minced GARLIC CLOVE
    3 Tbsp. OLIVE OIL
    4 Tbsp. VINEGAR
    1/2 tsp. SALT
    1/4 tsp. BLACK PEPPER
    1/2 tsp. crushed OREGANO

Toss first 6 ingredients together in a large bowl. In a jar, combine the dressing ingredients. Cover and shake vigorously until thoroughly mixed. Drizzle dressing over beans and vegetables. Toss well.

Creamy-yellow garbanzos, often referred to as "chickpeas", are a favorite of Spain and Portugal. Their nut-like flavor mixes well with other vegetables to create fabulous salads and appetizers.

Lima Supreme

2 lb. dried LIMA BEANS
1/2 lb. chopped BACON
1 finely chopped ONION
2 (6 oz.) cans TOMATO PASTE
1 Tbsp. DRY MUSTARD
SALT & PEPPER to taste
1/2 lb. BROWN SUGAR

Soak beans overnight. Cook beans, bacon and onion for 45 minutes to 1 hour. Beans will be firm. Transfer to a large roaster. Add tomato paste, mustard, salt and pepper. Cover and bake at 300 degrees for 1 hour. Remove lid, add sugar and brown slowly, stirring and adding water until well browned, about 4 hours or until desired consistancy.

Baby limas are actually the dry form of fresh green limas. They can be used in most recipes calling for "white beans."

Baked Lima Beans

2 cups dried BABY LIMA BEANS, cooked
1/4 cup BUTTER
1/2 cup BROWN SUGAR
2 Tbsp. KETCHUP
1 Tbsp. MUSTARD
1/2 cup HEAVY CREAM

Combine first 5 ingredients. Fold in cream. Put in a greased 2 quart casserole dish. Bake, uncovered, at 350 degrees for 45 minutes.

Black Bean Relish

2 (15 oz.) cans BLACK BEANS, drained
1 medium RED ONION, diced
1 diced TOMATO
1 chopped BELL PEPPER
1 Tbsp. SALAD OIL
1 Tbsp. VINEGAR
3 Tbsp. SALSA
1/2 tsp. GARLIC SALT

Combine all of the ingredients together and mix well. Cover and chill for 1 hour.

Black Beans
with Rice

2 (15 oz.) cans BLACK BEANS, drained
2 cups cold cooked RICE
1 chopped stalk CELERY
1 sliced GREEN ONION
1 medium chopped TOMATO
1/4 cup OLIVE OIL
1/4 cup LEMON JUICE
1 minced GARLIC CLOVE
1/2 tsp. SALT
1/8 tsp. BLACK PEPPER
1/8 tsp. TABASCO® SAUCE

In a large bowl, combine beans, rice, celery, green onion and tomato; mix well. In a small bowl, whisk remaining ingredients together and fold into beans, rice and vegetable mixture. Cover and refrigerate 1 hour to blend flavors.

Barbecued Lima Beans

2-4 slices of BACON
1 chopped ONION
1 finely chopped clove GARLIC
1 Tbsp. FLOUR
1 cup SPICY TOMATO JUICE
1/2 tsp. DRY MUSTARD
2 Tbsp. BROWN SUGAR
1 tsp. WORCESTERSHIRE SAUCE
2 cups cooked LIMA BEANS

Fry the bacon in a skillet and let drain on paper towel. Pour off drippings from the skillet reserving about 2 tablespoons. Sauté onion and garlic in the reserved drippings until brown. Blend in flour gradually and slowly stir in the tomato juice. Add mustard, brown sugar and Worcestershire sauce. Cook for 5 minutes. Add lima beans and pour into a 2-quart casserole dish. Top with the crumbled bacon pieces and bake in a 400 degree oven for 30 minutes.

Legumes provide protein, calcium, phosphorus, vitamins and other nutrients that are vital for good health.

Charro Beans

Charro beans are served whole in their cooking juices.

1/2 lb. PINTO or PINK BEANS
1/2 chopped ONION
2 minced GARLIC CLOVES
6 cups WATER
1 JALAPEÑO or ANAHEIM CHILE PEPPER
1/2 lb. lean cooked HAM, cubed
1 cup SALSA
SALT & PEPPER to taste

Combine beans, onion, garlic and water in a large pot and bring to a boil. Lower heat, cover pot and let the beans simmer for about 2 hours or until tender. Cut slits in the sides of the jalapeño pepper and add it and the other remaining ingredients to the beans. Cook uncovered for another 20 minutes over low heat.

One cup of cooked or canned beans supplies 12 to 15 grams of vegetable protein, depending on the variety.

Bean-Stuffed Potatoes

1 Tbsp. BUTTER
1 Tbsp. CHILI POWDER
1/2 tsp. GARLIC SALT
2 sliced GREEN ONIONS
1 (4 oz.) can diced GREEN CHILES
1 (15 oz.) can drained or 2 cups cooked
    PINTO BEANS
4 large hot BAKED POTATOES
1/2 cup shredded CHEDDAR CHEESE
SOUR CREAM

In a saucepan, heat butter until melted. Add chili powder, garlic salt, green onions and green chiles. Sauté for about 1 minute. Stir in beans and heat thoroughly. Split potatoes lengthwise and using a fork, fluff the potatoes. Spoon equal amounts of the bean mixture over the potatoes. Top with shredded cheese and a dollop of sour cream.

Acid slows the cooking process, so always wait to add tomatoes or vinegar until beans are almost done. The calcium in molasses has the same effect.

Fava Beans

2 cups dried FAVA BEANS
1 chopped ONION
2 minced GARLIC CLOVES
2 chopped TOMATOES
juice of 1 LEMON
2 Tbsp. OLIVE OIL
1/2 tsp. OREGANO
SALT & PEPPER to taste

Soak beans overnight covered in water. Replace with fresh water the next day. Bring to a boil, then turn down heat and simmer until beans are tender. Drain and add remaining ingredients. Mix thoroughly until half of the beans are broken.

Spanish Lentils

2 cups cooked LENTILS
1 chopped ONION
1 (15 oz.) can STEWED TOMATOES
1 chopped GREEN BELL PEPPER
2 Tbsp. OIL
1 tsp. OREGANO
1/2 tsp. SWEET BASIL
1/4 tsp. GARLIC SALT
1 1/2 tsp. CORNMEAL

Combine all of the ingredients in a skillet being careful that the cornmeal doesn't become lumpy. Simmer on low heat until onion and green pepper are tender.

Chilibeans

Cover **one pound (2 cups) DRIED PINK BEANS or KIDNEY BEANS** with boiling water and let stand for an hour or so. Drain beans and put into a large, heavy pot, cover with boiling water again and add:

1 chopped ONION
2-3 minced GARLIC CLOVES
1/3 cup BACON DRIPPINGS or COOKING OIL
1 1/2 tsp. SALT
1 (8 oz.) can TOMATO SAUCE
1 1/2 tsp. CHILI POWDER
1/4 tsp. CUMIN

Cover and cook slowly for about three hours, until beans are tender and a rich sauce has formed. Add more hot water if necessary. Beans should be neither too dry nor too juicy.

Luau Beans

4 cups cooked GREAT NORTHERN BEANS
1 chopped ONION
1/2 lb. cooked HAM, cubed
1 (15 oz.) can PINEAPPLE CHUNKS, drained
1/2 cup packed BROWN SUGAR
1/2 cup KETCHUP
2 Tbsp. PREPARED MUSTARD

Combine ingredients together and mix well. Pour into a greased 13 x 9 x 2 inch baking dish. Cover and bake for 1 1/2 hours in a 350 degree oven. Uncover and bake for an additional 20 minutes.

Southwestern
Red Beans

2 cups dried RED BEANS
1/4 cup SALSA
1/2 cup TOMATO PURÉE
1/2 tsp. CHILI POWDER
1/2 tsp. GROUND CUMIN
1 tsp. SALT
dash of DRY MUSTARD

After soaking, wash beans and drain. Place beans in cooking pot with enough water to cover at least 4 inches above the beans. Simmer over medium-low heat for two hours or until tender, add more water if needed. Do not boil rapidly, as skins will burst. Add remaining ingredients and simmer 20 minutes more.

Small red beans are a cousin of the kidney and Aduki beans. They are bush-type beans with smooth-bordered, heart-shaped leaves and white, yellow or purple flowers.

Limas in Red Sauce

2 cups dried LIMA BEANS
1 chopped ONION
1 diced medium TOMATO
1 cup TOMATO PURÉE
2 minced GARLIC CLOVES
1 tsp. SALT
PEPPER to taste

Wash and drain beans in a colander. Place limas in cooking pot and cover with water 4 inches above beans. Bring to a boil and reduce heat to medium-low, cooking for about 2 hours or until tender. Add more water if needed. During the last 1/2 hour of cooking, add the remaining ingredients.

Lima beans are in the kidney bean family. Two main types are available: the large, thick-seeded "potato" limas which are cream-colored and mellow-tasting and the small seeded "baby" lima beans which are green.

Rice & Kidney Beans

1 lb. dried KIDNEY BEANS
2 Tbsp. VEGETABLE OIL
SALT PORK, HAM or SAUSAGES
2 minced GARLIC CLOVES
1/2 tsp. THYME
SALT & PEPPER to taste
2 Tbsp. BUTTER
1 lb. RICE, washed

Cover kidney beans with water and bring to a boil until beans are soft. Drain off water and save. Heat oil in a large frying pan. Add beans and cut up meat and fry until slightly browned. Add bean water, and if insufficient, add boiling water to equal 4 cups liquid. Add garlic, thyme, salt and pepper. Heat to a rapid boil and add butter and rice. Continue to boil until rice has absorbed most of the mixture. Then reduce heat and cover, simmering over a very low heat until rice is cooked and beans are tender.

Beans can be soaked overnight or several hours prior to cooking. Do not salt soaking water as this will make the skin of the beans tough.

Columbian Black Beans

The milk floating on top makes this dish uniquely different.

1 lb. dried BLACK BEANS
SALT to taste
2 Tbsp. COOKING OIL
1 chopped ONION
BLACK PEPPER to taste
MILK

Wash beans well and soak overnight in cold water. In the morning, drain and cover again with cold water. Slowly bring to boiling point. Add salt to taste and allow to simmer until beans are tender.

Heat cooking oil in a frying pan. Fry the chopped onion until it is browned. Add drained beans with a dash of black pepper. Turn beans in oil until coated. Add just enough milk to cover. Bring slowly to a boil and serve.

Lentils & Rice Casserole

1 cup dried LENTILS
1 cup uncooked RICE
1/4 cup BUTTER
4 chopped PLUMS
1 chopped GREEN APPLE
1 finely chopped ONION
1 tsp. SALT
1/2 tsp. CINNAMON

Preheat oven to 350 degrees. Cook lentils and rice separately as packages direct. Drain lentils and rice and toss together in a large bowl. In a skillet, melt butter and cook plums, onion and apple until soft. Add to lentil/rice mixture. Mix in remaining ingredients. Spoon into a greased 2-quart casserole and cover. Bake 40 minutes.

Bean Stuffing

*For great Southwestern flavor, try this
unique stuffing!*

1 lb. CHORIZO (a spicy Mexican sausage)
1 lb. PORK SAUSAGE
1 chopped ONION
2 (15 oz.) cans PINTO BEANS, drained
1/4 tsp. GARLIC POWDER
3 Tbsp. minced, fresh PARSLEY
1 tsp. SAGE
1 (9 oz.) bag CORN CHIPS or TORTILLA CHIPS

Fry chorizo and sausage in a large skillet until thoroughly cooked. Drain very well. Sauté onions in the same frying pan. Return meats to pan and add beans, garlic powder, parsley and sage. Place chips in a large plastic bag, crush to break into small pieces. Add crushed chips to skillet and simmer all together for 15 minutes, stirring occasionally.

This recipe will stuff a 12-lb. turkey or can be baked in a greased casserole dish in a moderate oven until top is crispy and served as a side dish.

Great Northern Beans

2 cups dried GREAT NORTHERN BEANS
BAY LEAF
1 chopped GARLIC CLOVE
2 whole CLOVES
1/2 cup finely chopped ONION
3 Tbsp. OIL
1 finely chopped GREEN PEPPER
3 Tbsp. chopped, fresh PARSLEY

Soak beans overnight with bay leaf, garlic and 2 whole cloves. In the morning, remove bay leaf and two whole cloves and cook beans in the same water until tender (about 2 hours). Brown onion in oil, add green pepper and parsley and cook until tender. Add to the beans, mix thoroughly and serve.

Ham & Beans Aloha

1 (28 oz.) can BAKED BEANS
2 lb. fully cooked HAM STEAKS, cut into
bite-size pieces
3 PINEAPPLE RINGS, cut in halves
2 Tbsp. BROWN SUGAR

In a 2-quart casserole, combine beans and ham. Top with the pineapple slices and sprinkle with the brown sugar. Bake, uncovered, at 350 degrees for 30 minutes.

Apple & Navy Bean Casserole

This is a great combination of flavors!

2 cups dried NAVY BEANS
6 cups cold WATER
1 tsp. SALT
3 large APPLES, peeled and sliced
3/4 cup BROWN SUGAR
1/2 tsp. CINNAMON
1 1/2 Tbsp. BUTTER

Wash beans and soak overnight to cut down on cooking time. Drain the soaking water and cover with the 6 cups cold water. Add salt and bring to a boil. Turn down the heat to a simmer, cover and cook for an hour and 30 minutes. Drain the beans. Layer the beans and apples in a greased 2-quart casserole dish. Sprinkle the brown sugar and cinnamon over each layer. Dot with butter, cover and bake for 1 1/2 hours at 300 degrees.

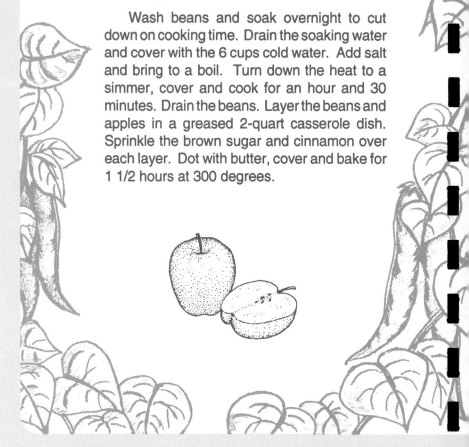

Hummus

Pronounced "hŭmmŭs". This Middle-Eastern favorite makes a great spread for crackers.

2 cups cooked
GARBANZO BEANS
1 GARLIC CLOVE
1/4 cup LEMON JUICE

1/4 cup OLIVE OIL
COLD WATER
FRESH PARSLEY

Purée first four ingredients in a food processor or blender. Add a little water, if needed to make mixture softer. Garnish with chopped fresh parsley on top and refrigerate for at least one hour before serving.

Bean Patties

2 cups cooked GREAT NORTHERN
    BEANS
1 tsp. APPLE CIDER VINEGAR
1 Tbsp. OIL
1/2 cup chopped ONION
1/2 tsp. OREGANO
2 Tbsp. chopped, fresh PARSLEY
1 EGG
CRACKER CRUMBS

Cook the beans and press through a food mill or sieve while still hot (they purée much better). Add remaining ingredients except for egg and cracker crumbs. Form bean mixture into patties, dip into beaten egg and then roll in cracker crumbs. Fry in hot oil or if you prefer, grease a baking pan with oil and bake at 425 degrees for 10 minutes or until brown, turning once. Serve hot!

Sweet & Tangy Beans

1 (16 oz.) can PORK & BEANS
1 (28 oz.) can BAKED BEANS with
    bacon and brown sugar
1 (23 oz.) can RANCH STYLE® BEANS
1 (4 oz.) can chopped GREEN CHILES
1 large, chopped ONION
3 large stalks chopped CELERY
1 chopped CARROT
1/4 cup BROWN SUGAR
2 + Tbsp. MOLASSES
1/4 cup BARBECUE SAUCE

Put all ingredients into a crock pot on LOW. Let simmer all day. If too much liquid remains at the end of cooking time, put in a large saucepan on stove and cook uncovered until desired thickness. Serve with brown or white rice.

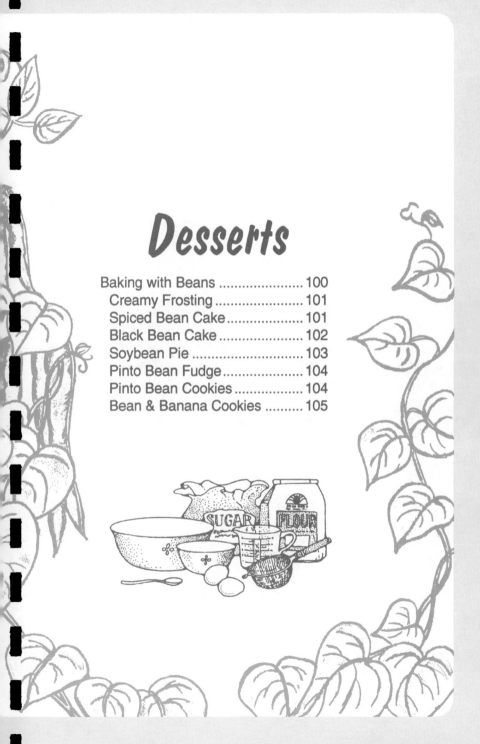

Desserts

Baking with Beans

Baking with puréed beans can be achieved by using your own home cooked beans or by using canned beans. If you are using your cooked beans, make sure they are well cooked and very tender with no flavorings added to the cooking water. Drain the beans thoroughly. Purée in a food processor until they reach a smooth and creamy consistency. If you are using canned beans, (they work perfectly fine) be sure to rinse and drain the beans thoroughly.

Baking with beans makes for a more moist and nutritious delight. Allow for longer baking times due to the added water content in the bean purée.

Spiced Bean Cake

2 cups BISCUIT MIX
1 1/2 cups SUGAR
1 tsp. CINNAMON
1/2 tsp. ALLSPICE
1/2 tsp. NUTMEG
1/3 cup softened BUTTER
2 EGGS
3/4 cup MILK
1 1/2 cups REFRIED BEANS
1/2 cup RAISINS
1/2 cup chopped NUTS

Preheat oven to 350 degrees. Combine biscuit mix, sugar, cinnamon, alspice and nutmeg. Add butter, eggs, and 1/4 cup milk. Mix at medium speed until well blended. Add refried beans, remaining milk, raisins and nuts. Beat well by hand and pour into a greased 8 x 8 x 2 pan. Bake in 350 degree oven for one hour or until firm. Serve warm or let cool and frost with **Creamy Frosting.**

Creamy Frosting

Add enough **WHIPPING CREAM** to 1 1/2 cups of **POWDERED SUGAR** to achieve a spreading consistency. Add 1/2 tsp. **VANILLA** 1/4 tsp. **CINNAMON** and a dash of **SALT.**

Black Bean Cake

1/4 cup BUTTER or MARGARINE
3 EGGS
1 tsp. VANILLA
2 cups cooked and puréed BLACK BEANS
1 cup FLOUR
1 tsp. BAKING SODA
1 cup SUGAR
1 tsp. CINNAMON
4 Tbsps. COCOA
1/2 cup chopped PECANS or WALNUTS
1 cup CHOCOLATE CHIPS

Cream butter, eggs and vanilla together. Stir in bean purée and beat well. Add all of the dry ingredients and combine thoroughly. Fold in the chopped nuts and chocolate chips. Pour into a greased 9 x 13 inch cake pan and bake at 375 degrees for 45-50 minutes. Frost with your favorite icing.

Soybean Pie

This pie tastes very much like pumpkin pie.

1 1/2 cups well-cooked **SOYBEANS**
3/4 cup **HONEY**
1 tsp. **CINNAMON**
1/2 tsp. **GINGER**
3/4 tsp. **NUTMEG**
2 slightly beaten **EGGS**
3/4 cup **MILK**
PREPARED PIE CRUST (your favorite
   recipe or frozen)

Preheat oven to 450 degrees. Puree soybeans in a blender or food processor. Combine with remaining ingredients except for the pie crust and pour into crust. Bake for 15 minutes, then reduce heat to 350 degrees and bake for an additional 30 minutes or until knife comes out clean. Delicious served with whipped topping.

Pinto Bean Fudge

1 cup cooked and mashed PINTO BEANS
3/4 cup softened BUTTER
3/4 cup COCOA
1 Tbsp. VANILLA
1/2 cup chopped WALNUTS
2 lbs. POWDERED SUGAR

Combine beans, butter, cocoa and vanilla together. Stir in nuts and powdered sugar. Batter will be stiff. Spread into a buttered 9 x 13 inch pan. When thoroughly chilled, cut in squares. Store in the refrigerator.

Pinto Bean Cookies

1 cup cooked and puréed PINTO BEANS
2 EGGS
1 cup SUGAR
1/2 cup BUTTER or MARGARINE, softened
2 cups FLOUR
1 tsp. BAKING SODA
1/2 tsp. SALT
1/2 tsp. CINNAMON
1 cup chopped NUTS
1 cup RAISINS

Preheat oven to 350 degrees. In a large mixing bowl, combine puréed beans, eggs, sugar and butter. Sift together the flour, baking soda, salt and cinnamon and blend into the bean mixture. Stir in the nuts and raisins. Drop by teaspoonful on a greased cookie sheet and bake for 15 minutes.

Bean & Banana Cookies

1 cup BROWN SUGAR
2 EGGS
1/2 cup BUTTER
1/2 tsp. VANILLA
3/4 cup cooked and puréed NAVY BEANS
1 mashed BANANA
1 tsp. BAKING SODA
1 3/4 cup FLOUR
1/2 cup QUICK COOKING OATS
1 cup CHOCOLATE CHIPS

Preheat oven to 375 degrees. Cream sugar, eggs, butter and vanilla together. Add beans and banana and beat until fluffy. Add baking soda, flour and oats. Blend till smooth. Stir in chocolate chips. Drop by teaspoonful onto greased cookie sheet. Bake for 15-20 minutes or until golden brown.

Note: Raisins substitute well for the chocolate chips.

Bean Festivals

Black-Eyed Pea Jamboree — Athens, TX (annual), 3rd weekend in July.   800-755-7878

California Dry Bean Festival — Tracy, CA (annual), 1st weekend in August.   209-835-2131

National Lentil Festival — Pullman, WA (annual), last weekend in August.   800-365-6948

Chile & Frijole Festival — Pueblo, CO (annual), September.   719-542-1704

Mountain View Bean Fest — Mountain View, AR (annual), Oct. 29-31.   501-269-8068

Index

About the Author

Living in the Southwest offers Shayne Fischer the opportunity to sample many new and exciting food trends. "I really enjoy experimenting with Southwestern foods and refining the many different combinations that are available," says Shayne, an active homemaker, writer and publisher.

An exercise enthusiast, Shayne combines her interest in foods that taste good with a desire to create recipes that are nutritious and healthy. "Most of us would live longer and happier lives if we paid more attention to what we eat and to getting regular, beneficial exercise."

Shayne was born and still lives in Arizona. Active in the family publishing business (Golden West Publishers) and community affairs, she and her husband, Lee, find time for power walking, running, bicycling and hiking. They have just completed two new cookbooks, *Low Fat Mexican Recipes* and *Vegi-Mex: Vegetarian Mexican Cookbook*.

SALSA LOVERS COOK BOOK

More than 180 taste-tempting recipes for salsas that will make every meal a special event! Salsas for salads, appetizers, main dishes, and desserts! Put some salsa in your life! By Susan K. Bollin.

5 1/2 x 8 1/2—128 pages . . . $5.95

QUICK-N-EASY
MEXICAN RECIPES

More than 175 favorite Mexican recipes you can prepare in less than thirty minutes. Traditional items such as tacos, tostadas and enchiladas. Also features easy recipes for salads, soups, breads, desserts and drinks. By Susan K. Bollin.

5 1/2 x 8 1/2—128 pages . . . $5.95

CHIP & DIP LOVERS
COOK BOOK

More than 150 recipes for fun and festive dips. Make southwestern dips, dips with fruits and vegetables, meats, poultry and seafood. Salsa dips and dips for desserts. Includes recipes for making homemade chips. By Susan K. Bollin.

5 1/2 x 8 1/2—112 pages . . . $5.95

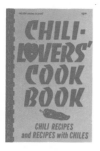

CHILI-LOVERS COOK BOOK

Chili cookoff prize-winning recipes and regional favorites! The best of chili cookery, from mild to fiery, with and without beans. Plus a variety of taste-tempting foods made with chile peppers. 150,000 copies in print! By Al and Mildred Fischer.

5 1/2 x 8 1/2—128 pages . . . $5.95

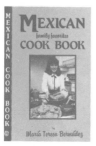

MEXICAN FAMILY FAVORITES
COOK BOOK

More than 250 easy-to-follow homestyle recipes for tacos, tamales, menudo, enchiladas, burros, salsas, frijoles, chile rellenos, carne seca, guacamole, breads and sweet treats! By Maria Teresa Bermudez.

5 1/2 x 8 1/2—144 pages . . . $6.95

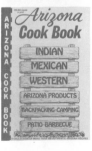

ORDER BLANK

GOLDEN WEST PUBLISHERS

☼ 4113 N. Longview Ave. • Phoenix, AZ 85014

602-265-4392 • **1-800-658-5830** • FAX 602-279-6901

Qty	Title	Price	Amount
	Arizona Cook Book	5.95	
	Best Barbecue Recipes	5.95	
	Chili-Lovers Cook Book	5.95	
	Chip and Dip Lovers Cook Book	5.95	
	Easy Recipes for Wild Game & Fish	6.95	
	Easy RV Recipes	6.95	
	Gourmet Gringo	14.95	
	Joy of Muffins	5.95	
	Low Fat Mexican Recipes	6.95	
	Mexican Desserts and Drinks	6.95	
	Mexican Family Favorites Cook Book	6.95	
	Quick-n-Easy Mexican Recipes	5.95	
	Real New Mexico Chile	6.95	
	Salsa Lovers Cook Book	5.95	
	Tequila Cook Book	7.95	
	Texas Cook Book	5.95	
	Tortilla Lovers Cook Book	6.95	
	Veggie Lovers Cook Book	6.95	
	Vegi-Mex Mexican Recipes	6.95	
	Wholly Frijoles! The Whole Bean Cook Book	6.95	

| Shipping & Handling Add ⮞ | U.S. & Canada | $3.00 | |
| | Other countries | $5.00 | |

☐ My Check or Money Order Enclosed $

☐ MasterCard ☐ VISA ($20 credit card minimum)

(Payable in U.S. funds)

Acct. No.   Exp. Date

Signature

Name   Telephone

Address

City/State/Zip

9/97   **Call for FREE catalog**   Wholly Frijoles!

This order blank may be photo-copied.